BUILDING *a*
CULTURE *of* DISTINCTION

BUILDING *a* CULTURE *of* DISTINCTION

PARTICIPANT WORKBOOK
for Defining Organizational Culture
and Managing Change

Sheila L. Margolis, PhD

**WORKPLACE
CULTURE
INSTITUTE**

©2010 Sheila L. Margolis
Workplace Culture Institute

ISBN: 978-0-9796657-1-4

For more information or materials on the
Building a Culture of Distinction Program,
go to *www.CultureofDistinction.com* or *www.SheilaMargolis.com*,
e-mail *smargolis@CultureofDistinction.com*
or call 404-255-8998.

Cover Design: George Foster
Interior Design and Production: Bill Groetzinger
Copyediting: Erica M. Rauzin

CONTENTS

Objectives

**To Build a Culture of Distinction
in your organization**

- Discuss the importance of culture, the Building a Culture of Distinction Program Cycle and the basics of the Five Ps (Introduction)

- Define the vital Purpose, distinctive and enduring Philosophy and strategic Priorities that constitute the Core Culture (Phase 1)

- Create a Core Culture Map with definitions, examples and stories, and a Core Culture Statement that identify and describe the Core Culture (Phase 1)

- Audit Practices and Projections to evaluate the degree of alignment of activities with the Core Culture (Phase 2)

- Develop a Core Culture Alignment Plan that lists actions to be taken, timeframe, person(s) responsible and resources needed to enhance the alignment of Practices and Projections with the Core Culture (Phase 3)

- Develop measures to monitor alignment of Practices and Projections with the Core Culture to gauge success in implementing the Core Culture Alignment Plan (Phase 3)

- Execute the plan and monitor progress in living the Core Culture principles (Phase 4)

- Conduct ongoing assessments, audits and revisions to the plan to ensure you are Building a Culture of Distinction (Conduct Updates)

INTRODUCTION

Objective
- Discuss the importance of culture, the Building a Culture of Distinction Program Cycle and the basics of the Five Ps

1. WHY IS CULTURE IMPORTANT TO YOU?

Overview

Successful leaders know the power of workplace culture. They unite employees around a small, compelling set of principles that generate business success. With an understanding of culture, you can create a workplace where people are doing the right work in an organization where they have a real sense of connection and belonging. The results: increased profits, and a thriving and dedicated workforce.

Using the framework of the Five Ps, you will be able to analyze your Core Culture, align it with your workplace practices and shape it, if necessary, to enhance your competitiveness. Culture is unique to each organization, and culture can contribute to – or detract from – achieving success. You must first understand your Core Culture before you can ensure that it supports your strategy and, thus, provides the foundation and framework for achieving your goals.

This Building a Culture of Distinction Program is the path to discovering and using your organization's hidden asset: its Core Culture. Through this program, you will learn how to define your Core Culture, create a customized Core Culture Map, and manage your culture using the Core Culture Audit and Alignment process.

Now, begin the journey to creating a workplace where everyone understands the Core Culture, personally connects to it and wants to live by it. Use this process to shape your culture and position the organization so you can compete and thrive.

Key Points about Culture

Culture influences behavior.
- Core Culture is often unspoken and goes unchallenged.
- Core Culture is powerful and can be difficult to change.

Culture and strategy are intertwined.
- Core Culture will either drive your strategy or sabotage it.
- Core Culture provides the foundation and framework for strategy; therefore, evaluate your Core Culture to be sure it supports your goals.

Core Culture is a collective mindset.
- Everyone in the organization must participate in defining the Core Culture.
- Everyone in the organization must understand the Core Culture, and be committed to living the Core Culture principles.

Core Culture is definable, measurable and moldable.
- Core Culture consists of the vital Purpose, the distinctive and enduring Philosophy and the strategic Priorities of the organization. During the culture-defining process, determine if aspects of the current Core Culture require change and assess the potential impact of those changes. The Core Culture must be genuine to the organization, and it must position the organization to be competitive and achieve its goals.
- Once you determine the Core Culture, evaluate the alignment of the organization's Practices and Projections to that Core Culture. What an organization says is valued should match the actions of its leaders and employees.
- Set measures to monitor how well you are living the Core Culture. Track your progress in aligning your actions to the Core Culture.

Manage your Core Culture to achieve results.

- Managing Core Culture is a core competency that all employees in an organization must understand.
- When employees know what is valued and their actions are aligned with the Core Culture, they are more productive—doing the right things—which supports achieving defined goals and, thus, succeeding in business.
- When employees understand the Core Culture and genuinely value the Core Culture attributes, they are more connected to the organization and more dedicated to its success.
- An organization becomes more adaptable and flexible when it knows which attributes to change and which ones to preserve.

Think for a Moment

- Are employees united around a small, compelling set of principles that drive success?
- Do employees flourish at work?
- Do you retain talent because they are connected to your organization, not just their jobs?

Creating a workplace this powerful begins with understanding culture.

Discussion Questions

1. Think about your organization's culture. What one aspect of it contributes the most to your business success?

    _____

    _____

    _____

    _____

    _____

    _____

    _____

    _____

    _____

2. What one aspect of your organization's culture would you like to change?

    _____

    _____

    _____

    _____

    _____

    _____

    _____

    _____

    _____

3. Describe the culture of an organization where you would want
    to work?

_____

_____

_____

_____

_____

_____

_____

_____

_____

_____

_____

_____

_____

_____

_____

_____

_____

2. PROGRAM CYCLE

This program will guide you in defining and managing your organizational culture. The program cycle includes the following phases: 1) define, 2) audit, 3) plan and 4) implement. The cycle must be continuously reviewed and evaluated to ensure that you are living the Core Culture principles that will generate success.

Phase 1: Define

Conduct a Core Culture Assessment to define your Core Culture.

Phase 2: Audit

Conduct a Core Culture Alignment Audit to identify the degree of alignment of the Practices and Projections with your Core Culture.

Phase 3: Plan

Develop a Core Culture Alignment Plan to guide you in making changes in your Internal Practices, External Practices and/or Projections to enhance their alignment with the Core Culture. Also, set measures to monitor alignment.

Phase 4: Implement

Execute and monitor the Core Culture Alignment Plan. Track and measure the organization's progress in implementing your action plan.

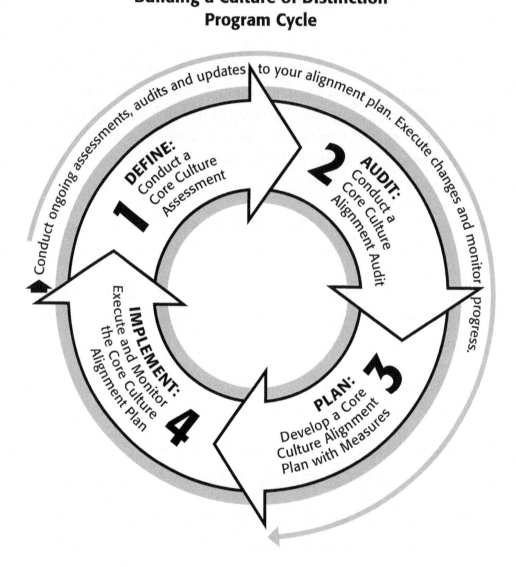

**Building a Culture of Distinction
Program Cycle**

Conduct ongoing assessments, audits and updates to your alignment plan. Execute changes and monitor progress.

1 DEFINE: Conduct a Core Culture Assessment

2 AUDIT: Conduct a Core Culture Alignment Audit

3 PLAN: Develop a Core Culture Alignment Plan with Measures

4 IMPLEMENT: Execute and Monitor the Core Culture Alignment Plan

3. THE BASICS OF THE FIVE Ps

The Central Three Ps of Core Culture: Purpose, Philosophy and Priorities

The central three Ps constitute the Core Culture of an organization. Core Culture is the essence of the organization. It consists of the organization's vital Purpose, distinctive and enduring Philosophy and strategic Priorities. As a unit, these elements form the foundation for why the organization is in business and the framework for how it conducts that business. Understanding the organization's Core Culture is a necessary step in strategic planning, and an essential step in positioning an organization to practice and project the principles that will deliver success.

The Central Three Ps of Core Culture

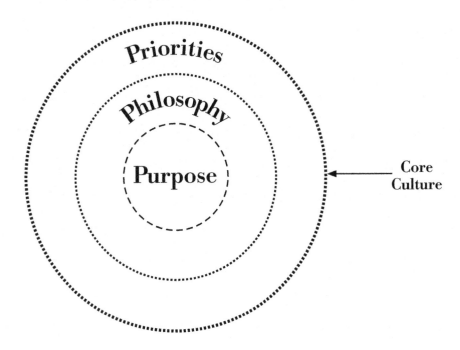

Core Culture and Strategy

Conducting a Core Culture Assessment to define your Core Culture is the first phase of a strategic planning process. Core Culture and strategy are intertwined. Your strategy must be aligned with your Core Culture, and your Core Culture must support your strategy. When they are in sync, your organization will be focused and positioned to accomplish the goals you envision. Core Culture provides the foundation and framework for the organization, and strategy provides the pathway for achieving success. If the organization's Core Culture does not support the strategy, then its efforts to achieve the strategy will be fragmented. Strategy does not succeed if it is not supported by a Core Culture that gives it the capability to execute. This is where most organizations fail. They have the strategy in place, but they lack the culture to nurture its realization. This link is vital and should never be neglected.

Core Culture and Strategy

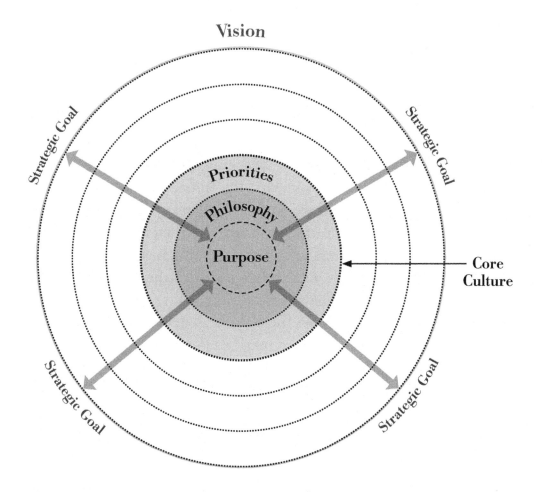

Alignment of the Five Ps

With an understanding of both your organization's Core Culture and its strategy, the path to success requires the alignment of the remaining Ps — Practices (Internal and External) and Projections — with the Core Culture and strategy.

Practices: Internal and External

- Internal Practices — These Practices include the inner workings of the organization that affect employee relationships, interactions and accomplishments. The Internal Practices—your organizational structure, work design and systems and processes for doing work; recruitment and selection; training and development; performance management; internal communications; and technology—must be aligned with the Core Culture and support your strategy.
- External Practices — These Practices define how the organization interacts with others outside the organization. The External Practices—your customers; the products and/or services you offer; suppliers, vendors and partners—must also be aligned with the Core Culture and the organization's strategy.

Projections

- These activities are the ways your organization paints an image of itself to the public. Projections include your organization's name; its logo and symbols; the image of your corporate headquarters and of your leader; the appearance of your offices and/or stores; the style of employee dress and uniforms; your marketing, public relations and advertising; and community activities. Your image should also align with your Core Culture and position your organization to achieve its goals.

Alignment of the Five Ps

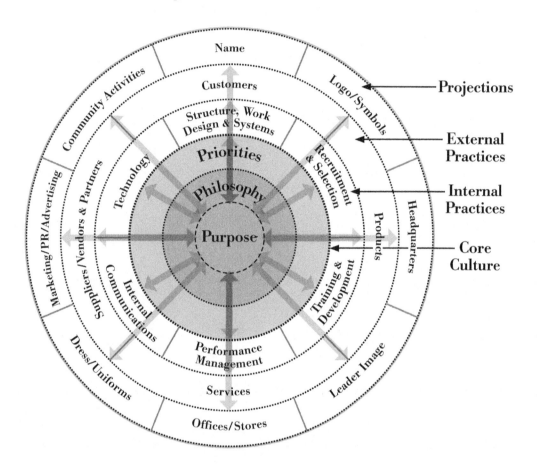

PHASE 1: DEFINE—
Conduct a Core Culture Assessment

Objectives

- Define the vital Purpose, distinctive and enduring Philosophy and strategic Priorities that constitute the Core Culture

- Create a Core Culture Map with definitions, examples and stories, and a Core Culture Statement that identify and describe the Core Culture

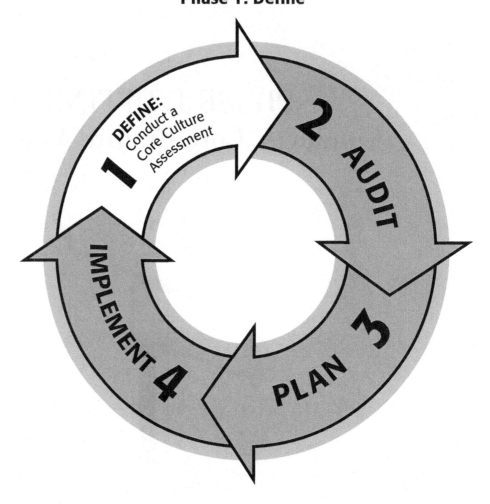

Building a Culture of Distinction
Program Cycle
Phase 1: Define

1. INTRODUCTORY ACTIVITY

1. Individually, complete the following:

● Write one thing about yourself—an interest, dream or aspiration—that others in the group probably do not know.

_____

_____

_____

_____

_____

● Write one word you would use to describe your organization. Give an example of it in practice.
Word:

_____

Example: _____

_____

_____

_____

_____

_____

2. Partner with someone you do not know well and take turns sharing responses.

3. Each person introduces his or her partner to the full group.

4. Discuss responses with the full group.

2. AN OVERVIEW OF PURPOSE

Overview

The Purpose is the most central component of Core Culture. The Purpose defines why the organization exists. The Purpose is not the answer to the question "What do you do?" which typically focuses on products, services and customers. Instead, it is the answer to the question "Why is the work you do important?" This may sound like a simple question, but in its simplicity is significance for the organization and for each employee.

The Purpose should be a statement that is inspirational and motivational. When the Purpose is meaningful to an employee, it provides a connection to work that is not just rational: it's also emotional. The Purpose is the cause that defines one's contribution to society. Businesses exist to make a profit, but they also exist to make a difference. Through work, individuals can make a difference and be part of a meaningful legacy.

A Purpose statement should be brief in length while broad in scope. Make it brief so employees can remember it and use it to guide their daily actions. Additionally, the Purpose should be broad in scope to allow the organization to adapt over time to a changing world while its central focus remains constant. Products and services often change, but the Purpose endures. Organizations are living entities; they are vehicles for improving life and the world we live in.

The Purpose is at the heart of the organization. Having a connection to the organization's Purpose is a driver of employee engagement.

Key Points about Purpose

The Purpose of the organization is the fundamental reason why the organization exists.

- Purpose is central and enduring to the culture of the organization.
- Purpose is the cause that defines one's contribution to society.
- Purpose unites efforts and inspires action.
- Purpose is the answer to the question: Why is this work important?
- A Purpose statement is brief in length and broad in scope.

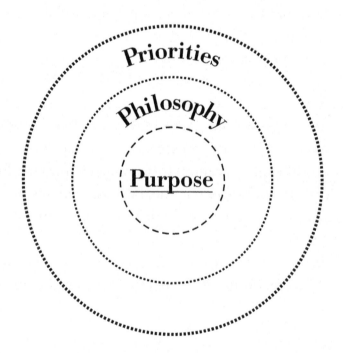

**Purpose:
"Why" Is This Work Important?**

Examples of Purpose Statements

Bank	We help people achieve their dreams
Beverage Company	We benefit and refresh
Bread Company	We nourish life
Communications Company	We enhance image
Entertainment Company	We make people happy
Food Company	We nurture health and well-being
Internet Company	We connect people to possibilities
Medical Group	We preserve and improve human life
Non-profit	We reduce poverty

Criteria for a Purpose Statement

The Six Purpose Criteria

- Is it a contribution to society—not a product or service?
- Does it answer the question…Why is this work important?
- Is it inspirational and motivational?
- Does it use powerful words?
- Is it brief in length so employees will remember it?
- Is it broad in scope to allow for future opportunities and change?

Activity: Defining the Purpose

1. In pairs, take turns asking these Purpose questions. Write your partner's responses below each question.

- What is the purpose of our organization? _____
  _____
  _____
  _____

- Why is that important?_____
  _____

- Why is that important?_____
  _____

- Why is that important?_____
  _____

- Why is that important?_____
  _____

- Why is that important?_____
  _____

  (Yes, ask up to five times. Each response moves you closer to the Purpose.)

  The Purpose is: _____
  _____
  _____

2. When requested, provide your pair's Purpose statement(s). The facilitator will list them on a flip chart. Many Purpose statements are short sentences consisting of the pronoun "we," a verb and a direct object.

Purpose Statement Options

3. As a full group, discuss and expand the list of Purpose statement options.

4. In small groups, list all Purpose statement options in the left column. Circle **Yes** or **No** to indicate if each Purpose statement option meets each of the six criteria. Discuss options and select the best Purpose statement.

Purpose statement options to be evaluated	Is a contribution to society—not a product or service?	Answers the question... Why is this work important?
	Yes No	Yes No
	Yes No	Yes No
	Yes No	Yes No
	Yes No	Yes No
	Yes No	Yes No
	Yes No	Yes No
	Yes No	Yes No
	Yes No	Yes No
	Yes No	Yes No

Is inspirational and motivational?	Uses powerful words?	Is brief in length?	Is broad in scope?
Yes No	Yes No	Yes No	Yes No
Yes No	Yes No	Yes No	Yes No
Yes No	Yes No	Yes No	Yes No
Yes No	Yes No	Yes No	Yes No
Yes No	Yes No	Yes No	Yes No
Yes No	Yes No	Yes No	Yes No
Yes No	Yes No	Yes No	Yes No
Yes No	Yes No	Yes No	Yes No
Yes No	Yes No	Yes No	Yes No

The Purpose statement chosen by the small group: _____

_____

_____

5. The facilitator will collect all Purpose statements chosen by each small group and list them on a flip chart. Discuss options and decide the Purpose statement for the organization.

Purpose Statement Options

The Purpose of our organization is: _____

_____

_____

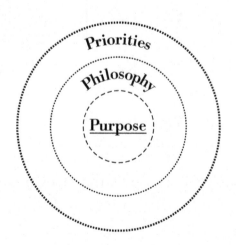

3. AN OVERVIEW OF PHILOSOPHY

Overview

In the model of the Five Ps, just outside of the Purpose is the organization's Philosophy. Where the Purpose states "why" the organization exists, the Philosophy directs "how" employees do their work. And "how" you do work matters. The Philosophy directs behavior across the organization. In successful organizations, employees consistently use the Philosophy to guide their decisions and daily actions.

The Philosophy may be one value or a small set of values. Of course, many values may feel important, but the Philosophy is only the value or values that are fundamental, distinguishing and enduring to the organization. They are the beliefs that have been essential and core to the character of the organization over the years. Employees believe that their Philosophy distinguishes their organization from others, particularly those which fulfill a similar Purpose. And the Philosophy is the enduring core beliefs that should never change. The Philosophy is extremely important.

The Philosophy is like the personality or character of the organization. This character is typically derived from the organization's founder, or from the principles and ideals that drove the organization's creation.

The Philosophy is what employees believe in today, what was most important in the past and what will continue to be important in the future. Where the Purpose is the heart of the organization, the Philosophy is its soul.

Key Points about Philosophy

The Philosophy of the organization is a value or small set of values that are fundamental, distinguishing and enduring to the organization. The Philosophy directs how employees do their work.

- The Philosophy is those special attributes derived from the founder that have influenced the character of the organization.
- Philosophy is the source of the organization's distinctiveness.
- The Philosophy provides the enduring framework for "how" employees do their work.

Philosophy:
"How" Is Your Organization Distinctive?

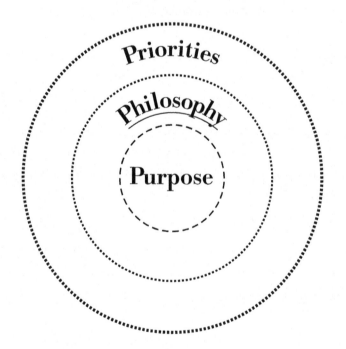

Criteria for a Philosophy

The Five Philosophy Criteria

- Is it a prime value?
- Does it guide "how" we do our work?
- Is it a source of our distinction?
- Is it derived from the organization's founder or the ideals that drove the organization's creation?
- If changed, would that alter the character of the organization?

Activity: Defining the Philosophy

1. Individually, answer the following questions:

a. What prime value is fundamental and distinctive to your or-
    ganization? _____
    _____
    _____

    Describe the value. _____
    _____

    Give an example of the value in practice. _____
    _____
    _____

b. What special attribute does the organization's founder possess
    that has influenced the character of the organization? _____
    _____
    _____

    Give a story that illustrates that attribute. _____
    _____
    _____
    _____
    _____

2. Share your responses with another person. Together, decide
    what you believe is the Philosophy of your organization.

    The Philosophy is: _____
    _____
    _____

3. Present the Philosophy chosen by each pair to the full group.
   The facilitator will list all responses on a flip chart.

Philosophy Options

4. As a full group, cluster responses that are similar.

5. Discuss responses, including definitions, examples and stories
   that illustrate each Philosophy option.

6. List Philosophy options in the left column. In small groups, circle **Yes** or **No** to indicate if each Philosophy option meets each of the five criteria. Then, decide the Philosophy.

Philosophy options to be evaluated	Is it a prime value?	Does it guide "how" we do our work?
	Yes No	Yes No
	Yes No	Yes No
	Yes No	Yes No
	Yes No	Yes No
	Yes No	Yes No
	Yes No	Yes No
	Yes No	Yes No
	Yes No	Yes No
	Yes No	Yes No

Is it a source of our distinction?	Is it derived from the organization's founder or the ideals that drove the organization's creation?	If changed, would that alter the character of the organization?
Yes No	Yes No	Yes No
Yes No	Yes No	Yes No
Yes No	Yes No	Yes No
Yes No	Yes No	Yes No
Yes No	Yes No	Yes No
Yes No	Yes No	Yes No
Yes No	Yes No	Yes No
Yes No	Yes No	Yes No
Yes No	Yes No	Yes No

The Philosophy chosen by the small group: _____

_____

_____

_____

7. The facilitator will collect all Philosophy options chosen by the small groups and list them on a flip chart.

Philosophy Options

8. As a full group, discuss options and decide the Philosophy of
   the organization. The Philosophy should be a value or small set
   of values.

   The Philosophy of our organization is: _____
   _____
   _____
   _____

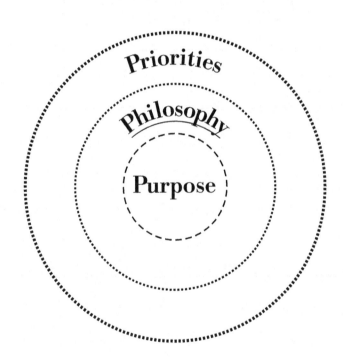

9. Give your Philosophy a label or title such as the Company Philosophy, the Company Principles, the Company Standards, the Company Way (insert company name) or whatever title is most appropriate for your organization. List the value(s) and their definition(s). Then, convert the value(s) and definition(s) into principles. Principles often include the definitions in the statement. Only have a small number of principles that will be easy to remember. The Philosophy principles will be the statements that are discussed regularly. Compile examples and stories that illustrate the Philosophy principles.

Philosophy Title	
Value(s)	
Definition(s)	
Principles	
Examples and Stories	

4. AN OVERVIEW OF ORGANIZATIONAL IDENTITY

Overview

The Purpose and the Philosophy are the identity of the organization. As a unit, they are the central attributes that have defined the character of the organization and the cause that it has served over the years. The elements of Organizational Identity serve as the basis for all aspects of the business.

Any change to either the Purpose or the Philosophy will have a significant impact on the organization and its employees. Preserve these attributes. Only change them with a clear understanding that this is monumental change required for survival. When you alter either the Purpose or the Philosophy, the organization will feel like a different organization. Employees will need to reevaluate their connections to it, and many Practices and Projections will need to be altered.

Key Points about Organizational Identity

Together, the Purpose and the Philosophy constitute Organizational Identity.

Organizational Identity = Purpose + Philosophy

- Organizational Identity is the enduring essence of an organization.
- The organization's identity is the unique product of its history —not something that can be copied from others. It must be authentic.
- Organizational Identity serves as the anchor that grounds an organization and the filter through which employees screen their actions.
- Any change to the Purpose or the Philosophy can have a major impact on the organization and its employees.

The Purpose and the Philosophy Are Organizational Identity

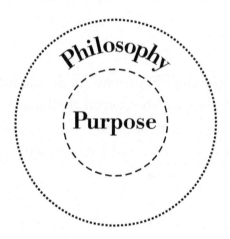

Discussion Questions

1. What would this organization be like if the Purpose changed?

   _____

   _____

   _____

   _____

2. What would this organization be like if the Philosophy changed?

   _____

   _____

   _____

   _____

3. Should either the Purpose or the Philosophy change? Explain.

   _____

   _____

   _____

   _____

5. AN OVERVIEW OF PRIORITIES

Overview

Priorities are the third component of Core Culture, yet not a part of Organizational Identity. Priorities are the strategic values that guide "how" the Purpose and the Philosophy are put into practice. Priorities position the organization to achieve its strategic goals. Only a few Priorities should be central to all areas of the organization. Those few values must support the Purpose and the Philosophy as well as the strategy. Evaluate Priorities based on how well they will contribute to a successful, thriving organization.

Priorities are relatively stable, but you can change them to enhance your organization's ability to compete. When your organization is undergoing change, consider altering its Priorities instead of its Purpose or Philosophy. Changing Priorities is a significant change, but it does not tamper with the personality or character of the organization, as long as any new Priorities are aligned with the Purpose and the Philosophy.

Key Points about Priorities
The Priorities of the organization are the strategic values that enable the organization to achieve its goals.

- Priorities are the standards for behavior that guide how the Purpose and Philosophy are put into practice.
- Priorities are limited to a small number of key values that are important to all areas of the organization.
- Priorities are those few values that, when followed by everyone, will enhance the competitiveness of the organization and enable it to thrive.
- Priorities are relatively stable, but they can be altered to keep your organization competitive, just as long as any new Priorities are consistent with the Purpose and the Philosophy.

Priorities:
What Values Will Help the Organization
Compete and Thrive?

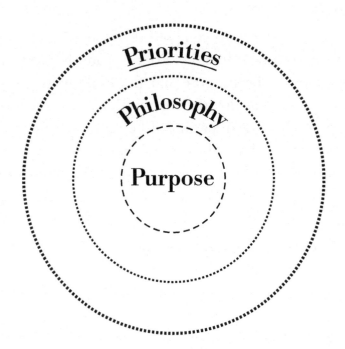

Criteria for a Priority

The Five Priority Criteria

- Is it a key value and important standard to guide behavior?
- Is this value important to all areas of the organization?
- If we abide by this value, will we enhance our ability to compete and thrive?
- Is this value aligned with the Purpose and the Philosophy?
- Does this value support our strategy?

Activity: Defining the Priorities

Priority Activity Option #1
(works best with groups of at least 15 people)

1. The facilitator will distribute a card to each person. Write on one side of the card:
   - A Priority that everyone must live by so the organization can compete and thrive.
   - An example of how that value could be put into practice.

The back of the card will have items numbered 1 through 4 with a place to indicate a number of points for each. It also has a place labeled "Total Points" with a corresponding blank.

Content on Card

Front of Card

- What is a Priority that all in the organization must live by if we want to compete and thrive?
  _____

- Provide an example of that value in practice. _____
  _____

Back of Card

1. _____ Points
2. _____ Points
3. _____ Points
4. _____ Points

Total Points: _____

2. Pair with Person #1.
   - Each person shares the value and example on his or her card.
   - Together, each pair distributes seven points between the two cards (only use integers, not fractions). Write the number of points on the back of each card.
   - Switch cards with your partner. (You no longer have your card.)

3. When instructed, pair with a second person. Continue the process with your new card.

4. The facilitator will instruct when to go to a new partner. If you get your original card, do not reveal that it's your card.

5. After the 4th pairing, go back to your seat and tabulate the number of points on the card you are holding.

6. The facilitator will collect Priorities—starting with the highest possible number of points (28) and counting backwards—and list Priority options on the flip chart. Discuss results. Cluster responses that are similar.

Priority Options	Points

7. List Priority options in the left column. Individually, circle **Yes** or **No** to indicate if each Priority option meets each of the five criteria. Then, as a full group, discuss the options. Those that do not meet the criteria should be removed from the list. Select the top Priorities (no more than three).

Priority options to be evaluated	Is it a key value and important standard to guide behavior?	
	Yes	No
	Yes	No
	Yes	No
	Yes	No
	Yes	No
	Yes	No
	Yes	No
	Yes	No
	Yes	No

Is this value important to all areas of the organization?		If we abide by this value, will we enhance our ability to compete and thrive?		Is this value aligned with the Purpose and the Philosophy?		Does this value support our strategy?	
Yes	No	Yes	No	Yes	No	Yes	No
Yes	No	Yes	No	Yes	No	Yes	No
Yes	No	Yes	No	Yes	No	Yes	No
Yes	No	Yes	No	Yes	No	Yes	No
Yes	No	Yes	No	Yes	No	Yes	No
Yes	No	Yes	No	Yes	No	Yes	No
Yes	No	Yes	No	Yes	No	Yes	No
Yes	No	Yes	No	Yes	No	Yes	No
Yes	No	Yes	No	Yes	No	Yes	No

The Priorities of our organization are:

Priority–_____

Priority–_____

Priority–_____

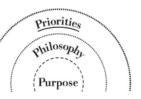

8. In small groups, compile definitions of each Priority with examples and stories illustrating each Priority.

Priority			
Definition			
Examples			
Stories			

9. In the full group, the facilitator collects definitions, examples and stories. Determine the best definition for each Priority, and compile examples and stories that illustrate each Priority.

Priority			
Definition			
Examples			
Stories			

Priority Activity Option #2
(works with groups of any size)

1. Individually, answer the question:
    What must we do to compete and thrive?

    _____

    _____

    _____

    _____

    _____

    _____

    _____

    _____

    _____

    _____

2. In small groups, share and compile responses. Then, consolidate the list, clustering ideas that are similar.

What must we do to compete and thrive?

3. In small groups, transfer the results to the left column of the table. Then, discuss what values are inherent to each response, and list them in the next column. Provide a definition of each value.

What must we do to compete and thrive?	

What value is the basis for this practice?	Definition of value

4. In small groups, list the values as the Priority options in the left column. Circle **Yes** or **No** to indicate if each Priority option meets each of the five criteria. Those that do not meet the criteria should be removed from the list.

Priority options to be evaluated	Is it a key value and important standard to guide behavior?
	Yes No
	Yes No
	Yes No
	Yes No
	Yes No
	Yes No
	Yes No
	Yes No
	Yes No

Is this value important to all areas of the organization?	If we abide by this value, will we enhance our ability to compete and thrive?	Is this value aligned with the Purpose and the Philosophy?	Does this value support our strategy?
Yes No	Yes No	Yes No	Yes No
Yes No	Yes No	Yes No	Yes No
Yes No	Yes No	Yes No	Yes No
Yes No	Yes No	Yes No	Yes No
Yes No	Yes No	Yes No	Yes No
Yes No	Yes No	Yes No	Yes No
Yes No	Yes No	Yes No	Yes No
Yes No	Yes No	Yes No	Yes No
Yes No	Yes No	Yes No	Yes No

5. In small groups, select the top three Priorities that meet the criteria. Rank them 1, 2 and 3 and write them in the left column of the appropriate row. Include definitions.

Top Three Priorities	Definition	Ranking
		#1
		#2
		#3

6. Small groups report their top three Priorities, with definitions and rankings, to the full group. The #1 choice receives 5 points, #2 choice receives 3 points and #3 choice receives 1 point. The facilitator combines points for Priorities that repeat from other groups. Discuss the top Priorities and how they meet the five criteria. Ensure that these Priorities, if followed, position the organization to achieve its strategic goals. Determine the top Priorities—typically no more than three.

Priorities	Definition	Rank #1 (5 pts.)	Rank #2 (3 pts.)	Rank #3 (1 pt.)	Total Points

The Priorities of our organization are:

Priority—_____

Priority—_____

Priority—_____

Priorities

Philosophy

Purpose

7. List the organization-wide Priorities. Decide the best definition for each Priority. Discuss examples of each and share stories that illustrate those Priorities. Compile results in the table.

Priority	
Definition	
Examples	
Stories	

6. AN OVERVIEW OF CORE CULTURE

Overview

Core Culture is made up of the vital Purpose, distinctive and enduring Philosophy and strategic Priorities of your organization. Think of Core Culture as your hidden asset because through culture, you can create a community of workers who understand the uniqueness of their work and the valued contributions that they make.

As a product of the Core Culture Assessment process, you will construct a Core Culture Map that depicts the Core Culture attributes of your organization. Support that visual with definitions, examples and stories. Also, develop a Core Culture Statement that is easy to remember so employees keep the Core Culture in mind as they live it on a daily basis.

Your Core Culture is the basis for your differentiation. With a clear picture of who your organization is, distinctively, as illustrated through your Core Culture, everyone in your organization can share the goal of living those attributes in a collection of many different ways. Continuously reinforce the unique combination of attributes that define you and position you to be successful. This unique combination of traits serve as a filter to direct action. Of course, effective human resource practices, a smart strategy and competent execution are essential. Avoid copying your rivals. Instead, understand the strengths of your Core Culture, and be your best self, as an organization, each day in all that you do. Continuously introduce systems and practices that reflect the Core Culture principles. That will be your clearest path to success.

Once you have defined your Core Culture, communicate it to everyone in the organization. Share the results of the process that informed the decision making. Employees are often interested in details so communicate as much as you can and give regular updates.

After communicating the Core Culture, explain the next steps in the process — conducting the Core Culture Alignment Audit, and then developing and implementing the Core Culture Alignment Plan.

Key Points about Core Culture

Core Culture = Purpose + Philosophy + Priorities

- The powerful pairing of the Purpose and the Philosophy supported by the Priorities form the Core Culture of your organization.

- Core Culture is the essence of your culture and the basis for all action.

- Core Culture defines the prime principles that guide the organization.

- Core Culture is your hidden asset.

- With an understanding of Core Culture, you can build a community of workers who understand the uniqueness of their work and take pride in the valued contributions that they make.

Core Culture Products

Compile the following products:

1. Core Culture Map

Create a visual symbol of the Core Culture elements.

2. Definitions

Define each attribute to provide a rich understanding of the meaning of these Core Culture elements.

3. Examples

List practices for each attribute. These examples illustrate ways that leaders and employees can live the Core Culture attributes. These attributes are more than just words. Core Culture principles and values are meaningless if they are not infused in your workplace practices and demonstrated through everyone's behavior.

4. Stories

Collect stories that illustrate each attribute. Stories bring the attributes to life. Use them to share the Core Culture attributes with others. Stories are effective communication tools, and they are particularly useful in employee orientations.

5. Core Culture Statement

Create a short statement that captures the essence of the Core Culture. This statement is helpful in communicating and in promoting unity among employees around the Core Culture.

Activity: Constructing the Core Culture Statement

1. In small groups, review the company's Core Culture. Write the organization's name and the Purpose, Philosophy and Priorities on the appropriate lines of the Core Culture Map. Then, compile all the information in the table.

_____ **Core Culture Map**

Name of organization

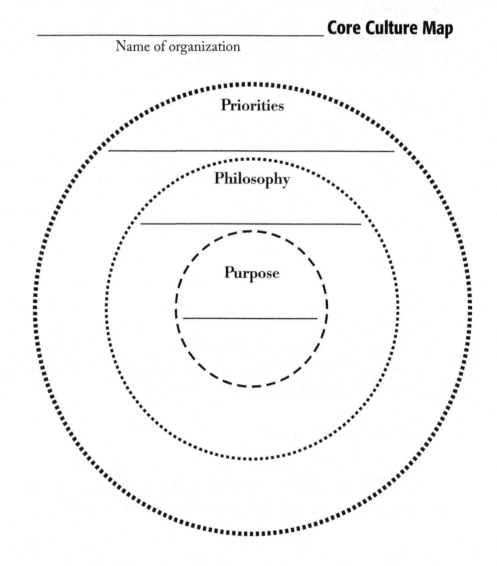

Core Culture	
Purpose (Statement)	
Philosophy (Title and Principles)	
Priorities (Values and Definitions)	

2. Then, in small groups, discuss options for a Core Culture Statement, and select the best short statement that captures the essence of the Core Culture.

Core Culture Statement Options

The Core Culture Statement chosen by the small group:

_____

_____

3. As a full group, the facilitator will collect all Core Culture
    Statements chosen by each small group and list them on a flip
    chart. Discuss options and decide the Core Culture Statement
    for the organization.

Core Culture Statement Options

The Core Culture Statement is:

_____

_____

PHASE 2: AUDIT –
Conduct a Core Culture Alignment Audit

Objective
- Audit Practices and Projections to evaluate the degree of alignment of activities with the Core Culture

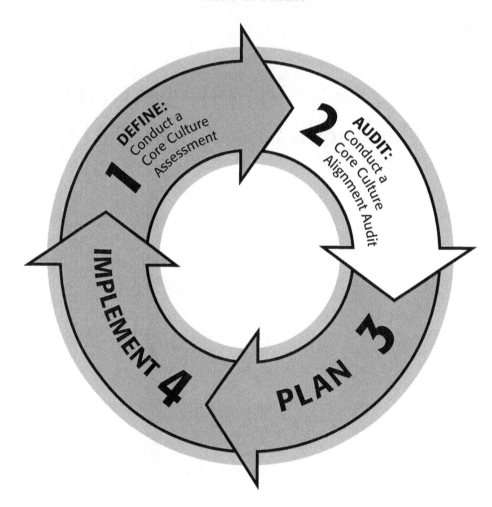

Building a Culture of Distinction
Program Cycle
Phase 2: Audit

1 DEFINE: Conduct a Core Culture Assessment

2 AUDIT: Conduct a Core Culture Alignment Audit

3 PLAN

IMPLEMENT 4

1. CORE CULTURE ALIGNMENT AUDIT

Overview

With the completion of the Core Culture Assessment, you can embark on the next phase: auditing how well your Practices and Projections are aligned with your Core Culture. To live the Core Culture that you have defined, you must align all aspects of the organization with it. When everyone understands the Core Culture and performs in ways that are consistent with it, the organization will be unified and geared for success.

To achieve alignment, the Purpose, the Philosophy and the Priorities must be embedded in all aspects of the organization, which are:

- The Internal Practices of the organization — how employees work with each other, including the structure, work design and systems and processes for doing work; recruitment and selection; training and development; performance management; internal communications; and technology;

- The External Practices of the organization — your customers, products, services, suppliers/vendors and partners; and

- The Projections of the organization — the images that the organization projects to the public through the name of your organization; logo and other corporate symbols; location of your corporate headquarters; image of the leader; design and appearance of your offices and stores; employees' dress or uniforms; marketing, public relations and advertising; and your community activities.

The Core Culture must also be aligned with and support your organization's strategy —its vision and strategic goals. This requires an inside/outside alignment process that contributes to consistent actions directed at stated goals. Employees should understand and value the attributes of the Core Culture, and each person's actions should be aligned with the Core Culture.

Conduct a Core Culture Alignment Audit to evaluate where gaps exist in your practice of the Core Culture principles. Decide upon the process you will use for auditing Internal Practices, External Practices and Projections, in terms of alignment with the Core Culture. This audit can be conducted by small employee groups, by a leadership team or through individual activities.

Aligning Practices and Projections with the Core Culture

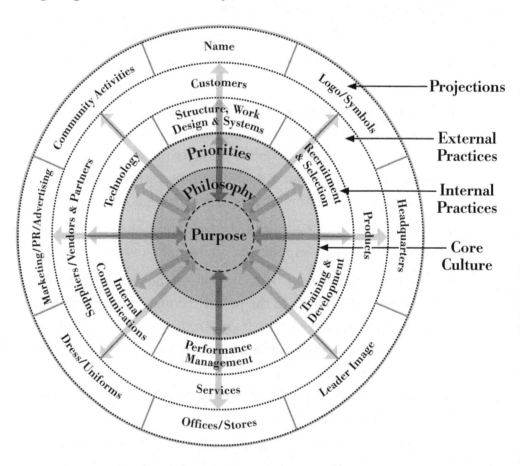

Key Points about a Core Culture Alignment Audit

All actions must be aligned with the Core Culture.

- Managing Core Culture requires periodic audits to evaluate the alignment of Internal Practices, External Practices and Projections with the Core Culture.

- Conducting a Core Culture Alignment Audit requires auditing the degree of alignment of each of the Internal Practices — structure, work design and systems and processes for doing work; recruitment and selection; training and development; performance management; internal communications; and technology — with the Core Culture.

- Conducting a Core Culture Alignment Audit requires auditing the degree of alignment of each of your External Practices — customers, products, services, suppliers/vendors and partners — with the Core Culture.

- Conducting a Core Culture Alignment Audit requires auditing the degree of alignment of each of the Projections — the name of your organization; logo and other corporate symbols; location of your corporate headquarters; image of the leader; design and appearance of your offices and stores; employees' dress or uniforms; marketing, public relations and advertising; and your community activities — with the Core Culture.

2. INTERNAL PRACTICES ALIGNMENT

Overview

Internal Practices are the internal workings of the organization that affect employee relationships, interactions and accomplishments. Because these Practices are closest to the Core Culture, the organization's consistency in aligning them with the Core Culture will have a major impact on organizational success.

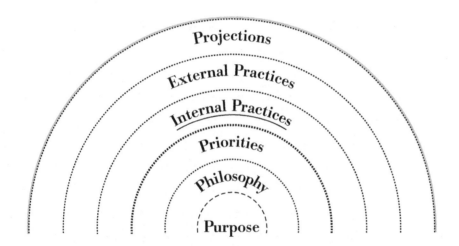

Internal Practices include organizational structure, work design and systems and processes for doing work. It encompasses your Practices in recruitment and selection; training and development; performance management; internal communications; and technology. The alignment process requires filtering each Internal Practice through the Core Culture. Your objective is to ensure that all of your organization's Practices support and reflect each attribute of the Core Culture. Managing Core Culture requires a commitment to performing Core Culture Alignment Audits to evaluate the organization's consistency in practicing the Core Culture principles.

If Internal Practices do not reflect the Core Culture attributes that the organization says it values, then the Core Culture will only be a collection of meaningless words.

Internal Practices to Be Aligned with the Core Culture

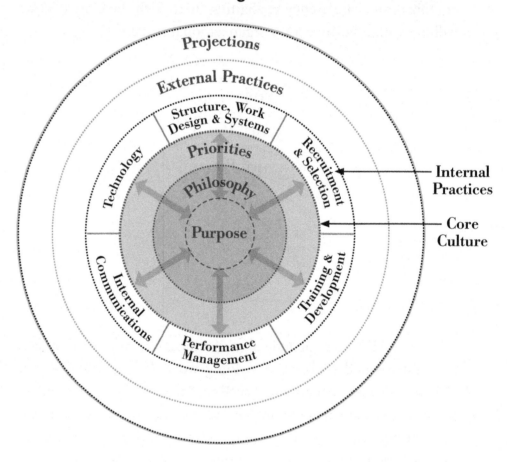

Key Points about Internal Practices Alignment

Alignment of Internal Practices with the Core Culture is essential for business success.

■ **Align Structure, Work Design and Systems with the Core Culture** — this includes the organization's structure, job titles, how work is organized, how decisions are made and the systems and processes for doing work.

- The structure of organizations can vary. Some are relatively static with clearly defined job descriptions and reporting structures with work organized around functions. Others are more fluid — where teams emerge on a short-term basis around projects, and job titles have little relevance. Ensure that your organization's structure, whatever it may be, aligns with and supports your Core Culture.

- Implement systems for doing work that reinforce and reflect the Core Culture. Employees' daily activities must be aligned with the Core Culture to keep it alive. Everyone must constantly work on improving systems so that Core Culture attributes are put into practice throughout the organization.

■ **Align Recruitment and Selection with the Core Culture**

- Finding the right people for your culture is a key component of an effective hiring process. Make rigorous efforts to ensure that candidates understand the Core Culture, personally connect with it and want to live by it. Use past actions and observable behaviors to gauge a candidate's genuine connection to the Core Culture attributes.

■ **Align Training and Development with the Core Culture**

- To retain talent, give new employees a quick start through a comprehensive orientation program that includes the Core Culture. Ensure that new employees understand the organization's Core Culture and how to practice its principles effectively. This foundational knowledge jumpstarts employee success on the job by inculcating the values that drive the organization and imparting the systems, processes and practices employees should follow to support the Core Culture. An effective Core Culture orientation helps new employees assimilate faster which promotes commitment and dedication. Your organization will yield high payoffs if it can retain valued employees. A Core Culture orientation includes an overview of the Five Ps and the organization's strategy. New employees should understand the Core Culture Map, and the definitions, examples and stories that clarify the Core Culture attributes. Employees must also understand how the Practices and Projections are linked to and aligned with the Core Culture. Effective orientations reduce costly turnover and have a positive impact on the bottom line.

- People want to develop and achieve through their work. When employees have opportunities for personal growth, they are more engaged in their work and more committed to the organization because it provides this development. Training is valuable for honing skills and enabling employees to live the Core Culture attributes at the expected high levels of performance. By helping employees increase their skills and build on their strengths, the organization enhances their individual worth and their ability to contribute to practicing the Core Culture attributes.

Align Performance Management with the Core Culture

- Clarifying performance standards allows employees to understand how they are evaluated so that their individual goals are clear. Living the Core Culture should be one area for evaluation. Create clear standards to measure how well employees practice Core Culture attributes. Link these personal goals and standards directly with the Core Culture and the measures established in the Core Culture Alignment Plan.

- Successful managers regularly communicate performance expectations, and provide feedback and support. Give positive feedback to employees when they model the behaviors that contribute to living the Core Culture principles. Recognizing employee contributions in a variety of ways that are meaningful to individual employees can build commitment and dedication to the organization.

Align Internal Communications with the Core Culture

- A two-way flow of information is essential for creating a feeling of inclusion and ownership. Employees should regularly talk about the Core Culture and how well they live it. Effective communication starts at the top with leaders who provide broad messages that flow throughout the organization, and supervisors who reinforce the message and apply it to the specifics of their group. Communication involves listening as well as providing information. Ongoing dialogue through a variety of media heightens the workforce's understanding of the Core Culture and its importance.

Align Technology with the Core Culture

- Technology should facilitate work, enabling effective, efficient practice of the Core Culture principles. A proper investment in software and equipment can facilitate living the Core Culture attributes and can provide data on how well you are practicing those prime principles.

3. EXTERNAL PRACTICES ALIGNMENT

Overview

External Practices define how your organization interacts with outsiders — those who are not employees. External Practices include your customers; the products and services that you offer to them; and your suppliers, vendors and partners. Align each of these areas with the Core Culture to create a positive impact on the Core Culture and your business.

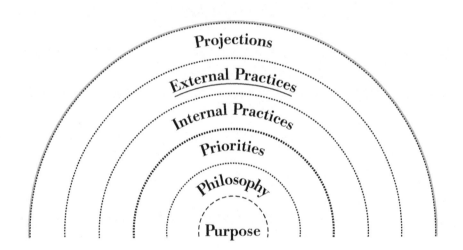

The alignment process requires filtering each External Practice through the Core Culture. Your objective is to ensure that all of your organization's External Practices support and reflect the Core Culture. Building a Culture of Distinction requires a commitment to performing an ongoing Core Culture Alignment Audit to evaluate your organization's consistency in practicing the Core Culture principles.

External Practices to Be Aligned with the Core Culture

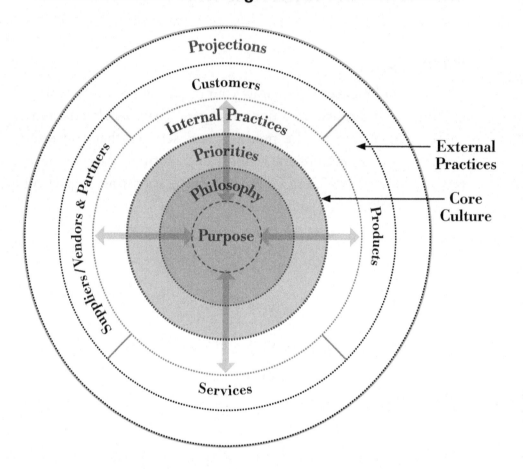

Key Points about External Practices Alignment

**Alignment of External Practices with the Core Culture is
essential for business success.**

■ **Align your Customers with the Core Culture**

- Target customer and market segments where you will best
  compete. Strengthen relationships through shared values.
  Assess past customers, current customers and potential customer groups. Build a customer base that understands and
  values your Core Culture.

■ **Align your Products and Services with the Core Culture**

- Reflect the traits that make you special in the products and
  services you offer. Don't limit yourself to current products
  and services. Be open to the variety of ways that you can
  work to achieve your Purpose. Be sure that the products and
  services you offer align with the Philosophy and the Priorities you value.

■ **Align your Suppliers, Vendors and Partners with the Core
Culture**

- Screen your suppliers, vendors and partners to ensure that
  they uphold the values that you hold dear. Shared interests
  and values ensure that your Core Culture will be strong.
  When conflicting values arise, act quickly to sustain the
  Core Culture attributes that matter to you. Manage relationships and activities to sustain your Core Culture.

4. PROJECTIONS ALIGNMENT

Overview

Projections are the final P in the Five Ps. Projections are not the substance of your Core Culture, but rather the reflections of the organization to the public. Projections include the name of your organization; its logo and other corporate symbols; the location of your corporate headquarters; the image of the leader; the design and appearance of your offices and stores; employees' dress or uniforms; marketing, public relations and advertising; and your community activities. Each of these areas must be aligned with the Core Culture to portray a portrait consistent with the Core Culture principles.

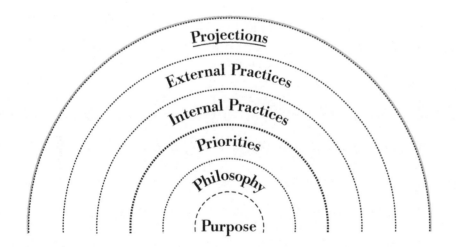

In most organizations, changes in Projections are easier to manipulate than changes in Practices. But Projections are very important internally and externally. Projections are symbolic and emotionally relevant to employees. Changes in Projections can have an impact on how employees feel about the organization. For example, a change in a symbol can have a dramatic effect on employees who are emotionally connected to the previous image. Projections also reflect the Core Culture to those outside the organization. Any inconsistencies between projected images and actual experiences can have a negative impact on your organization and your ability to drive business success.

The alignment process requires filtering each Projection through the Core Culture. Your objective is to ensure that all Projections support and reflect the Core Culture attributes. Building a Culture of Distinction requires a commitment to performing an ongoing Core Culture Alignment Audit to evaluate your organization's consistency in projecting the Core Culture principles.

Projections to Be Aligned with the Core Culture

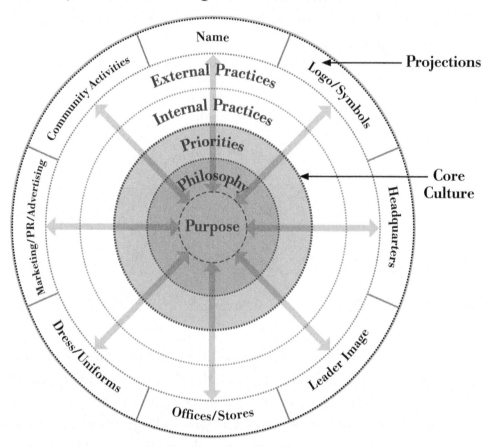

Key Points about Projections Alignment

Alignment of Projections with the Core Culture is essential for business success.

■ **Align your Organization's Name with the Core Culture**

- The organization's name is an important reflection of the organization to the public as well as a representation of its essence to employees. Ensure that your name reflects the Core Culture.

■ **Align your Logo and other Corporate Symbols with the Core Culture**

- Various symbols, including the logo and other images, are associated with your organization and used as images to express it. They must reflect ideals that align with the Core Culture.

■ **Align the Location of your Headquarters with the Core Culture**

- People associate many organizations with the location of their headquarters. Make sure the headquarters for your organization supports the image you choose to project.

■ **Align the Image Projected by the Leader with the Core Culture**

- The leader serves as a symbol of the organization. The image that the leader projects can affect people's perceptions of the organization. If that image does not reflect the Core Culture, it will lessen the value placed on the Core Culture attributes.

■ **Align the Design and Appearance of your Offices and Stores with the Core Culture**

- Employee offices and company stores are visual symbols of the culture. Be sure that they project your values.

■ **Align your Employee Dress and Uniforms with the Core Culture**

- Employee dress and uniforms are visual messages of the Core Culture, both internally and externally. They are a symbolic representation of the values of the organization.

■ **Align your Marketing, Public Relations and Advertising with the Core Culture**

- Marketing, public relations and advertising are designed to affect image and perception. Keep the Core Culture at the center of all of these efforts. Be sure that the image you project is consistent with your Core Culture.

- Monitor your internet image so that it accurately portrays your Core Culture principles.

■ **Align your Community Activities with the Core Culture**

- Evaluate your community activities based on their strategic contribution as well as the benefits they offer to the community. Choose community activities that reflect the Core Culture and contribute to your strategy.

5. ACTIVITY: CONDUCT A CORE CULTURE ALIGNMENT AUDIT

The audit phase requires a review of the alignment of each Core Culture attribute — the Purpose, the Philosophy and the Priorities — with each Internal Practice, External Practice and Projection.

1. List the organization's Purpose, Philosophy and Priorities at the top of each table.

2. Then, individually, for each question, circle the number that corresponds to the degree of alignment with each Core Culture attribute.

    The scale has five options:

           1 = Extremely Unaligned

           2 = Unaligned

           3 = Somewhat Aligned

           4 = Aligned

           5 = Extremely Aligned

    For areas requiring greater alignment, provide recommendations on how to enhance alignment.

3. When you have completed the audit, tabulate Core Scores and Item Scores. Core Scores will indicate the degree of alignment for each Core Culture attribute. Item Scores will show the degree of alignment for each question for all Core Culture attributes.

4. In small groups, discuss the alignment audit results. Compare scores with others in your group. Note the areas of strength and the areas that require action. Discuss recommendations of each group member.

Core Culture Alignment Audit Worksheet
Internal Practices Alignment Audit

STRUCTURE, WORK DESIGN & SYSTEMS						
1 = Extremely Unaligned 2 = Unaligned 3 = Somewhat Aligned 4 = Aligned 5 = Extremely Aligned						
	List each Core Culture attribute in a column below (Purpose, Philosophy, and Priorities)					
To what degree do the following align with the Core Culture…						**Item Score** (add scores for each row)
1. Does the organizational structure support the Core Culture?	1 2 3 4 5	1 2 3 4 5	1 2 3 4 5	1 2 3 4 5	1 2 3 4 5	
2. Do job titles reflect the Core Culture?	1 2 3 4 5	1 2 3 4 5	1 2 3 4 5	1 2 3 4 5	1 2 3 4 5	
3. Does the design of one's work reinforce the Core Culture?	1 2 3 4 5	1 2 3 4 5	1 2 3 4 5	1 2 3 4 5	1 2 3 4 5	
4. Do the systems for doing work align with the Core Culture?	1 2 3 4 5	1 2 3 4 5	1 2 3 4 5	1 2 3 4 5	1 2 3 4 5	
5. Does decision making reflect the Core Culture?	1 2 3 4 5	1 2 3 4 5	1 2 3 4 5	1 2 3 4 5	1 2 3 4 5	
RECRUITMENT & SELECTION						
6. Do recruitment materials reflect the Core Culture?	1 2 3 4 5	1 2 3 4 5	1 2 3 4 5	1 2 3 4 5	1 2 3 4 5	
7. Do recruitment practices support the Core Culture?	1 2 3 4 5	1 2 3 4 5	1 2 3 4 5	1 2 3 4 5	1 2 3 4 5	
8. Do you talk about the Core Culture with applicants?	1 2 3 4 5	1 2 3 4 5	1 2 3 4 5	1 2 3 4 5	1 2 3 4 5	
9. Do you model the Core Culture when meeting with applicants?	1 2 3 4 5	1 2 3 4 5	1 2 3 4 5	1 2 3 4 5	1 2 3 4 5	
10. Do you interview for culture fit?	1 2 3 4 5	1 2 3 4 5	1 2 3 4 5	1 2 3 4 5	1 2 3 4 5	
TRAINING & DEVELOPMENT						
11. Do you orient new employees to the Core Culture?	1 2 3 4 5	1 2 3 4 5	1 2 3 4 5	1 2 3 4 5	1 2 3 4 5	
12. Do you train new employees in the skills to be able to practice the Core Culture?	1 2 3 4 5	1 2 3 4 5	1 2 3 4 5	1 2 3 4 5	1 2 3 4 5	
13. Do you provide ongoing training to ensure actions meet/exceed standards for living the Core Culture?	1 2 3 4 5	1 2 3 4 5	1 2 3 4 5	1 2 3 4 5	1 2 3 4 5	
14. Does the way training is conducted model the Core Culture?	1 2 3 4 5	1 2 3 4 5	1 2 3 4 5	1 2 3 4 5	1 2 3 4 5	

continued on next page

PERFORMANCE MANAGEMENT						
1 = Extremely Unaligned 2 = Unaligned 3 = Somewhat Aligned 4 = Aligned 5 = Extremely Aligned						
	List each Core Culture attribute in a column below (Purpose, Philosophy, and Priorities)					
To what degree do the following align with the Core Culture…						**Item Score** (add scores for each row)
15. Do employees have standards for performance linked to the Core Culture?	1 2 3 4 5	1 2 3 4 5	1 2 3 4 5	1 2 3 4 5	1 2 3 4 5	
16. Do you hold employees accountable for personal action plans that reinforce the Core Culture?	1 2 3 4 5	1 2 3 4 5	1 2 3 4 5	1 2 3 4 5	1 2 3 4 5	
17. Do you give positive feedback to employees who model the Core Culture?	1 2 3 4 5	1 2 3 4 5	1 2 3 4 5	1 2 3 4 5	1 2 3 4 5	
18. Do you celebrate the achievement of goals that promote the Core Culture?	1 2 3 4 5	1 2 3 4 5	1 2 3 4 5	1 2 3 4 5	1 2 3 4 5	
INTERNAL COMMUNICATIONS						
19. Do you disseminate information about the Core Culture?	1 2 3 4 5	1 2 3 4 5	1 2 3 4 5	1 2 3 4 5	1 2 3 4 5	
20. Does the flow of information align with the Core Culture?	1 2 3 4 5	1 2 3 4 5	1 2 3 4 5	1 2 3 4 5	1 2 3 4 5	
21. Do leaders regularly talk about and demonstrate the Core Culture principles and values?	1 2 3 4 5	1 2 3 4 5	1 2 3 4 5	1 2 3 4 5	1 2 3 4 5	
22. Do meetings reflect the Core Culture?	1 2 3 4 5	1 2 3 4 5	1 2 3 4 5	1 2 3 4 5	1 2 3 4 5	
TECHNOLOGY						
23. Do you use equipment to support the Core Culture?	1 2 3 4 5	1 2 3 4 5	1 2 3 4 5	1 2 3 4 5	1 2 3 4 5	
24. Does your software effectively support the Core Culture?	1 2 3 4 5	1 2 3 4 5	1 2 3 4 5	1 2 3 4 5	1 2 3 4 5	
25. Does your intranet align with the Core Culture?	1 2 3 4 5	1 2 3 4 5	1 2 3 4 5	1 2 3 4 5	1 2 3 4 5	
Core Score (add scores for all questions in each column)						

continued on next page

Internal Practices Alignment Audit continued

Recommendations on How to Enhance Internal Practices Alignment

External Practices Alignment Audit

CUSTOMERS						
1 = Extremely Unaligned 2 = Unaligned 3 = Somewhat Aligned 4 = Aligned 5 = Extremely Aligned						
	List each Core Culture attribute in a column below (Purpose, Philosophy, and Priorities)					
To what degree do the following align with the Core Culture…						**Item Score** (add scores for each row)
1. Do your customers align with the Core Culture?	1 2 3 4 5	1 2 3 4 5	1 2 3 4 5	1 2 3 4 5	1 2 3 4 5	
2. Do your markets align with the Core Culture?	1 2 3 4 5	1 2 3 4 5	1 2 3 4 5	1 2 3 4 5	1 2 3 4 5	
PRODUCTS & SERVICES						
3. Do your products align with the Core Culture?	1 2 3 4 5	1 2 3 4 5	1 2 3 4 5	1 2 3 4 5	1 2 3 4 5	
4. Do your services align with the Core Culture?	1 2 3 4 5	1 2 3 4 5	1 2 3 4 5	1 2 3 4 5	1 2 3 4 5	
SUPPLIERS, VENDORS & PARTNERS						
5. Do your suppliers and vendors align with the Core Culture?	1 2 3 4 5	1 2 3 4 5	1 2 3 4 5	1 2 3 4 5	1 2 3 4 5	
6. Do your partners align with the Core Culture?	1 2 3 4 5	1 2 3 4 5	1 2 3 4 5	1 2 3 4 5	1 2 3 4 5	
Core Score (add scores for all questions in each column)						

Recommendations on How to Enhance External Practices Alignment

Projections Alignment Audit

NAME / LOGO & SYMBOLS					
1 = Extremely Unaligned　　2 = Unaligned　　3 = Somewhat Aligned　　4 = Aligned　　5 = Extremely Aligned					
	List each Core Culture attribute in a column below (Purpose, Philosophy, and Priorities)				
To what degree do the following align with the Core Culture…					**Item Score** (add scores for each row)
1. Does the organization's name reflect the Core Culture?	1 2 3 4 5	1 2 3 4 5	1 2 3 4 5	1 2 3 4 5	1 2 3 4 5	
2. Do the logo and symbols reflect and reinforce the Core Culture?	1 2 3 4 5	1 2 3 4 5	1 2 3 4 5	1 2 3 4 5	1 2 3 4 5	
HEADQUARTERS					
3. Does the location of your corporate headquarters align with the Core Culture?	1 2 3 4 5	1 2 3 4 5	1 2 3 4 5	1 2 3 4 5	1 2 3 4 5	
LEADER IMAGE					
4. Does the image of the leader align with the Core Culture?	1 2 3 4 5	1 2 3 4 5	1 2 3 4 5	1 2 3 4 5	1 2 3 4 5	
OFFICES & STORES / DRESS & UNIFORMS					
5. Does the appearance of your offices reflect the Core Culture?	1 2 3 4 5	1 2 3 4 5	1 2 3 4 5	1 2 3 4 5	1 2 3 4 5	
6. Does the appearance of your stores reflect the Core Culture?	1 2 3 4 5	1 2 3 4 5	1 2 3 4 5	1 2 3 4 5	1 2 3 4 5	
7. Does the dress/uniform of your employees support the Core Culture?	1 2 3 4 5	1 2 3 4 5	1 2 3 4 5	1 2 3 4 5	1 2 3 4 5	
MARKETING, PUBLIC RELATIONS & ADVERTISING					
8. Do your marketing activities align with the Core Culture?	1 2 3 4 5	1 2 3 4 5	1 2 3 4 5	1 2 3 4 5	1 2 3 4 5	
9. Do your PR activities align with the Core Culture?	1 2 3 4 5	1 2 3 4 5	1 2 3 4 5	1 2 3 4 5	1 2 3 4 5	
10. Does your advertising support the Core Culture?	1 2 3 4 5	1 2 3 4 5	1 2 3 4 5	1 2 3 4 5	1 2 3 4 5	
11. Do your internet activities align with the Core Culture?	1 2 3 4 5	1 2 3 4 5	1 2 3 4 5	1 2 3 4 5	1 2 3 4 5	

continued on next page

COMMUNITY ACTIVITIES

1 = Extremely Unaligned	2 = Unaligned	3 = Somewhat Aligned	4 = Aligned	5 = Extremely Aligned	

To what degree do the following align with the Core Culture…	List each Core Culture attribute in a column below (Purpose, Philosophy, and Priorities)					**Item Score** (add scores for each row)
12. Do your community activities align with the Core Culture?	1 2 3 4 5	1 2 3 4 5	1 2 3 4 5	1 2 3 4 5	1 2 3 4 5	
Core Score (add scores for all questions in each column)						

Recommendations on How to Enhance Projections Alignment

PHASE 3: PLAN–
Develop a Core Culture Alignment Plan with Measures

Objectives

- Develop a Core Culture Alignment Plan that lists actions to be taken, timeframe, person(s) responsible and resources needed to enhance the alignment of Practices and Projections with the Core Culture

- Develop measures to monitor alignment of Practices and Projections with the Core Culture to gauge success in implementing the Core Culture Alignment Plan

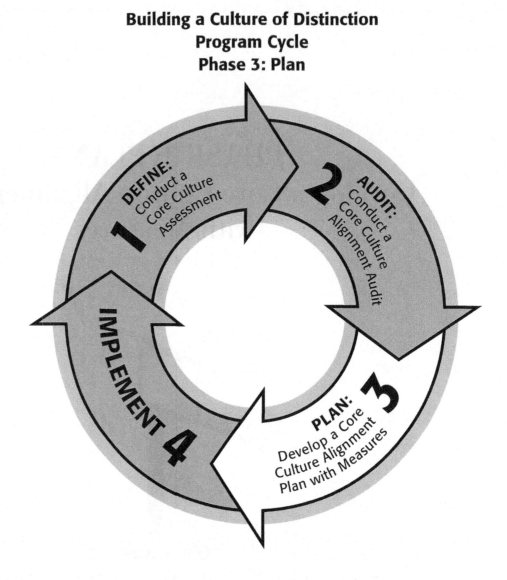

Building a Culture of Distinction
Program Cycle
Phase 3: Plan

DEFINE: Conduct a Core Culture Assessment 1

AUDIT: Conduct a Core Culture Alignment Audit 2

PLAN: Develop a Core Culture Alignment Plan with Measures 3

IMPLEMENT 4

1. CORE CULTURE ALIGNMENT PLAN WITH MEASURES

Overview

After you complete the Core Culture Alignment Audit, the next step is to create a plan for improving those areas of the organization that are not sufficiently aligned with the Core Culture. Your goal is to develop a plan that will remedy the gaps identified in the audit process. For each Practice and Projection category, review audit scores and recommendations, and then develop objectives to enhance alignment. For each objective, list the tactics that will accomplish the objective. For each tactic, provide the timeframe/due date for completing the tactic, the person(s) responsible and the resources needed.

A key component of the planning process is to create measures to monitor alignment. These measures will help you gauge if your actions are making the organization more successful in expressing the Core Culture principles. For example:

- Under the Internal Practice of Recruitment and Selection, you may have the objective: to screen applicants for their fit with the Core Culture. For this objective, you might choose "retention" as the variable to measure. By monitoring retention, you can determine if new hiring practices result in selecting employees who are committed to the organization and want to stay with it.

- An airline company that has service as a Core Culture attribute might have the objective—to improve the system for loading and unloading airplanes—under the Internal Practice of Structure, Work Design and Systems. For this objective, you might choose "turnaround time for flights" as the variable to measure. By monitoring turnaround time, you can determine if the new systems result in improved service.

Measures can vary in their content and nature. They could be an increased or decreased number, a percentage, a financial amount or a degree of change. They could be customer focused, like improved customer satisfaction, repeat business or increased referrals. They could relate to better business processes or practices that affect time, use of materials, sales or revenue. Whatever metrics you use, be sure that what you measure and how you measure it is clearly stated so that you can monitor the outcomes. By more effectively living the Core Culture, your organization will achieve results that improve its bottom line. Track progress and be sure that what you measure is linked to the results you desire.

Measures must also exist that are meaningful to each employee on a more frequent — even daily — basis. Employees must understand how they contribute to achieving desired goals "the Core Culture way." With daily actions that can be measured and individually monitored, each person can track how well he or she is making a meaningful contribution to living the Core Culture principles. Such measures can be incorporated into the performance management system.

Decide your process for developing the Core Culture Alignment Plan. You can conduct this process immediately following the audit or at a later session. Developing the plan should be a group effort focused on defining the organization's objectives. Integrate creative thinking into the process to find new and better ways to express the Core Culture. Set measures to use for monitoring performance to track alignment in living the Core Culture principles. When the Core Culture Alignment Plan is developed, share it with everyone in the organization.

Key Points about Developing a Core Culture Alignment Plan with Measures

A plan lists actions that must be taken to improve alignment with the Core Culture.

- Building a Culture of Distinction requires developing an alignment plan to specify objectives and actions that will improve alignment of Internal Practices, External Practices and Projections with the Core Culture.

- For areas that are out of alignment, create objectives to improve alignment.

- A Core Culture Alignment Plan includes a list of tactics for each objective, with the timeframe/due date, person(s) responsible and resources needed.

- Decide how you will monitor success in implementing the Core Culture Alignment Plan. Set metrics for evaluating progress.

- Reevaluate and adjust the plan to ensure that actions contribute to increased alignment in living the Core Culture.

2. ACTIVITY: DEVELOP A CORE CULTURE ALIGNMENT PLAN WITH MEASURES

Review the Core Scores and Item Scores and the recommendations to enhance alignment from the Core Culture Alignment Audit.

1. In small groups, discuss all the possible actions for improving alignment.

2. In the small group, develop a list of objectives that the group—as a whole—feels the organization should target for change. List the objectives by the appropriate category in the table.

Core Culture Alignment Plan: Initial Objectives

Internal Practices	
Categories	**Initial Objectives**
Structure, Work Design & Systems	
Recruitment & Selection	
Training & Development	
Performance Management	

continued on next page

Internal Practices *(continued)*	
Categories	**Initial Objectives**
Internal Communications	
Technology	

External Practices	
Categories	**Initial Objectives**
Customers	
Products	
Services	
Suppliers/Vendors & Partners	

continued on next page

Projections	
Categories	**Initial Objectives**
Name	
Logo/Symbols	
Headquarters	
Leader Image	
Offices & Stores	
Dress & Uniforms	
Marketing, Public Relations & Advertising	
Community Activities	

3. Present each small group's objectives to the full group or
   a leadership team. Discuss all objectives and decide which
   ones to include in your Core Culture Alignment Plan. List,
   in the table, objectives to be included in the alignment
   plan.

Core Culture Alignment Plan: Objectives

Internal Practices	
Categories	**Objectives**
Structure, Work Design & Systems	
Recruitment & Selection	
Training & Development	
Performance Management	

continued on next page

Internal Practices *(continued)*	
Categories	**Objectives**
Internal Communications	
Technology	

External Practices	
Categories	**Objectives**
Customers	
Products	
Services	
Suppliers/Vendors & Partners	

continued on next page

Projections	
Categories	**Objectives**
Name	
Logo/Symbols	
Headquarters	
Leader Image	
Offices & Stores	
Dress & Uniforms	
Marketing, Public Relations & Advertising	
Community Activities	

4. Preferably in small groups, complete a plan for assigned objectives. Specify the tactics under each objective. Note the expected timeframe/due date, the person(s) responsible and the resources needed. Duplicate this table and create a plan for each objective.

Core Culture Alignment Plan

Objective:			
Tactics	**Due Date**	**Person(s) Responsible**	**Resources Needed**

5. Next, in the small groups, decide if there are items you should measure. Create a measurement plan that details how you will gather information, how you will share that information and how you will use the data to evaluate success.

Core Culture Alignment Plan: Measures
Small Group

Aspects to Measure	Measurement Plan*

How information is gathered, shared and used to evaluate success

6. Share each small group's results with the full group or the leadership team (whoever will be making the decision on the plan and measures).

7. In the full group or leadership team, review the objectives and tactics. Prioritize actions based on strategy and resources. Update the Core Culture Alignment Plan to reflect the group's decision.

8. Decide a small number of measures to track. Don't measure everything. Only measure what will drive desired change. Update the aspects to measure and measurement plan in the table.

Core Culture Alignment Plan: Measures
Full Group/Leadership Team

Aspects to Measure	Measurement Plan

PHASE 4: IMPLEMENT –
Execute and Monitor the Core Culture Alignment Plan

Objective
- Execute the plan and monitor progress in living the Core Culture principles

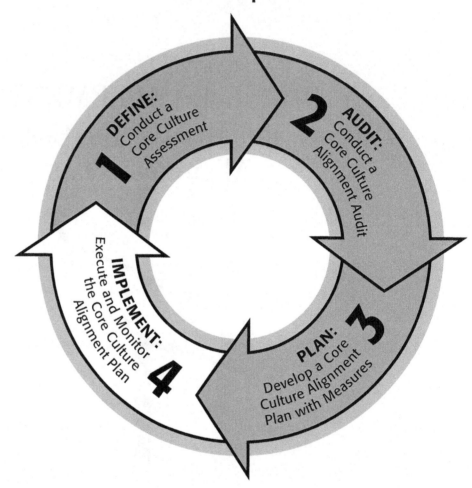

Building a Culture of Distinction
Program Cycle
Phase 4: Implement

1. EXECUTE AND MONITOR THE CORE CULTURE ALIGNMENT PLAN

Overview

Now, the Core Culture Alignment Plan is complete, and you are ready to implement it. The goal is to get better at living the Core Culture principles. If you are succeeding at meeting this goal, future alignment audits will indicate your organization's actions are more aligned with the Core Culture. Use the metrics you have established to judge how successful the organization is during this process.

First, share the alignment plan with everyone in the organization. Be sure everyone understands the plan, the importance of making these changes and how the organization will monitor progress. Communicate the scope of change and the underlying stability of the Core Culture as the basis for change. Communication must be clear, consistent and repetitive. It should be offered through a variety of methods and be ongoing. Verbal communication is essential on multiple levels. Supplement your oral messages with consistent written messages.

Everyone must see that the goal to "Align actions to the Core Culture" has a significant impact on everyone in the organization. Therefore, each person must understand his or her role in the plan and how he or she will contribute. Individuals should incorporate relevant plan objectives in their performance management objectives, and in the performance standards that relate to their work and responsibilities.

Use the measures and measurement plan to monitor progress in living the Core Culture principles. Communicate progress throughout the organization. Everyone should work to live the Core Culture more effectively, and should track his or her contribution to these efforts. Celebrate as you reach goals, and incorporate periodic activities that boost the organization's momentum in the process.

Key Points about Executing and Monitoring the Core Culture Alignment Plan

Execute the Core Culture Alignment Plan.

- Effectively communicate the Core Culture Alignment Plan so employees understand and feel ownership in living the Core Culture on a daily basis.

- Everyone in the organization must seek to improve how well he or she practices and projects the Core Culture principles.

- The goal is to execute the Core Culture Alignment Plan so that future alignment audits will indicate that Practices and Projections more consistently reflect the Core Culture.

- Everyone must be accountable for aligning his or her actions with the Core Culture.

- When everyone works to live the Core Culture more effectively, you have harmony in action.

Monitor alignment by tracking measures.

- Monitor performance in living the Core Culture principles using set measures.

- Communicate how well the organization is living the Core Culture.

- Individual performance management plans must incorporate clear performance standards linked to alignment measures.

- Everyone should be working to live the Core Culture more effectively, and each individual should be tracking his or her contribution to these efforts.

2. ACTIVITY: EXECUTE AND MONITOR THE CORE CULTURE ALIGNMENT PLAN

Develop a communication plan to share the Core Culture Alignment Plan and measures.

1. Use the table to map your communication strategy for sharing the Core Culture Alignment Plan and measures with everyone in the organization.

Communication Plan to Begin Implementation

Message	Audience	Timing	Medium*

* The way you choose to communicate your message

2. Use the table to plan how you will communicate progress in implementing the Core Culture Alignment Plan.

Communication Plan Throughout Implementation

Times to Share Progress	Audience	Frequency	Medium

3. Track the Core Culture Alignment Plan measures to monitor your progress in accomplishing objectives. Use the table to track the status of your progress and make recommendations to enhance alignment.

Core Culture Alignment Plan Measures: Status

Measures	Status	Recommendations

CONDUCT UPDATES

Objective

- Conduct ongoing assessments, audits and revisions to the plan to ensure you are Building a Culture of Distinction

**Building a Culture of Distinction
Program Cycle
An Ongoing Cycle**

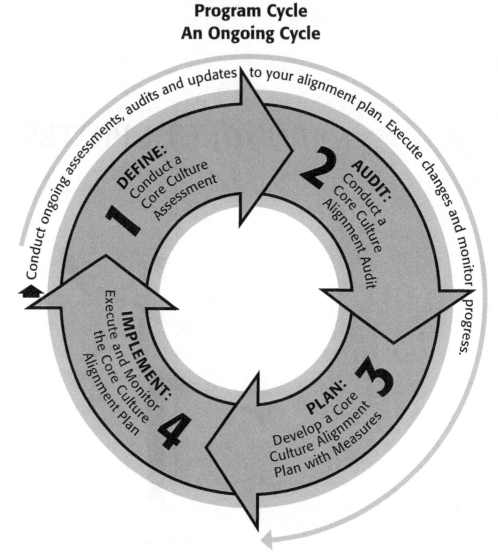

Conduct ongoing assessments, audits and updates to your alignment plan. Execute changes and monitor progress.

1 DEFINE: Conduct a Core Culture Assessment

2 AUDIT: Conduct a Core Culture Alignment Audit

3 PLAN: Develop a Core Culture Alignment Plan with Measures

4 IMPLEMENT: Execute and Monitor the Core Culture Alignment Plan

1. AN ONGOING CYCLE

Overview

As the program cycle illustrates, Building a Culture of Distinction is an ongoing process. Periodically reevaluate the Core Culture to ensure that the words and descriptions identifying the Core Culture attributes accurately capture the principles that define the character of the organization and will position it to compete and thrive. You may find that as your culture becomes more aligned, it may be harder to shift in a different direction. The strength of alignment can potentially build resistance to change. Always be conscious of this, and promote a framework that supports adaptability. Successful organizations must be self-reflective and able to objectively evaluate the need for change. Do not deter from building a strong culture. Instead, understand alignment and the multi-faceted approach to managing change so you will have the knowledge and tools to make change happen.

Make ongoing efforts to audit progress, identify gaps in alignment and act to improve the alignment of the Internal Practices, External Practices and Projections with the Core Culture. As new steps are needed to improve alignment, integrate those objectives into the Core Culture Alignment Plan with appropriate measures. As the organization's strategy changes, Priorities may change, altering the Core Culture. The plan might require adjustments. Don't wait for the next formal review of the plan to make alterations. Consider this program to be a living plan that you monitor and update. Track performance through established measures. Communicate progress and celebrate success.

Core Culture management is an ongoing responsibility of the leadership and a requirement for all employees in the organization. Everyone must be a participant in the change process. Employees must understand and feel ownership in defining the Core Culture and living it on a daily basis. The drivers of change must start at the top, but they must also be pushed from the bottom up. Unless people in all areas of the organization and on all levels genuinely value the Core Culture principles and see them as a basis for organizational success and personal success, they will not feel sufficient momentum on an ongoing basis to keep the strategic focus. Communication in a variety of forms and settings supports this process. Having leaders who sustain the Core Culture and hiring people who naturally value the Core Culture principles are the greatest insurance that your culture will thrive. If you accurately define the Core Culture and employees act in alignment with it, then your organization will be positioned to achieve its goals.

Key Points about Conducting Updates

Managing culture is an ongoing process.

- As the Building a Culture of Distinction Program Cycle illustrates, this process is iterative. Institute ongoing efforts to ensure that the Core Culture is valid and that all aspects of the organization have been audited to identify and solve gaps.

- Periodically reevaluate the Core Culture to ensure that the words and descriptions of the Core Culture attributes accurately capture its identity and the values that will position the organization to be competitive.

- As the organization needs to take new action to improve alignment, integrate those objectives into the Core Culture Alignment Plan with appropriate measures.

2. SUMMARY

Now you have the tools you need: a defined Core Culture and a plan to ensure that the Five Ps are in alignment. You are positioned to face the future knowing that everyone in your organization understands the importance of the Core Culture and is working individually and as part of the organizational community to support the shared principles that enable you to achieve desired goals. When you feel this degree of synchronization, value it and use that momentum to move you forward. And if you ever feel that the spirit is beginning to slip, seek to remedy any cause, immediately recharge it, and keep your Core Culture strong and successful.

CPSIA information can be obtained
at www.ICGtesting.com
Printed in the USA
BVOW08s1310280917
496086BV00002B/9/P